Chapter 1: Introduction to Financial Ratios

Financial ratios are a set of tools used by investors, analysts, and managers to evaluate the financial health and performance of a company. These ratios provide a standardized way to measure a company's financial performance and compare it with similar companies or industry benchmarks.

There are various types of financial ratios, each measuring a different aspect of a company's financial position. The most commonly used financial ratios include:

1. Profitability ratios: These ratios measure a company's ability to generate profit from its operations. Examples include gross profit margin, net profit margin, and return on assets.

2. Liquidity ratios: These ratios measure a company's ability to meet short-term financial obligations. Examples include current ratio and quick ratio.

3. Solvency ratios: These ratios measure a company's ability to meet long-term financial obligations. Examples include debt-to-equity ratio and interest coverage ratio.

4. Efficiency ratios: These ratios measure a company's efficiency in managing its assets and liabilities. Examples include inventory turnover ratio and receivables turnover ratio.

5. Market value ratios: These ratios measure a company's market value relative to its financial performance. Examples include price-to-earnings ratio and market-to-book ratio.

Financial ratios are generally calculated using data from a company's financial statements, including the income statement, balance sheet, and statement of cash flows. These ratios can provide insights into a company's financial health, such as its profitability, liquidity, and solvency.

However, it's important to keep in mind that financial ratios have limitations and should not be used in isolation to make investment or business decisions. Other factors, such as industry trends, company strategy, and market conditions, should also be considered.

In the following chapters, we'll dive deeper into each type of financial ratio and explore how they can be used to evaluate a company's financial performance. We'll also discuss common mistakes to avoid when using financial ratios and best practices for effective financial ratio analysis.

Chapter 2: Profitability Ratios

Profitability ratios are a group of financial ratios that measure a company's ability to generate profit from its operations. These ratios are used to evaluate a company's ability to earn profits relative to its sales, assets, and equity. Here are some of the most commonly used profitability ratios:

1. Gross profit margin: This ratio measures a company's profit after deducting the cost of goods sold (COGS) from its

revenue. It is calculated by dividing gross profit by revenue and multiplying the result by 100. A higher gross profit margin indicates that a company is generating more profit from its sales.

2. Net profit margin: This ratio measures a company's profit after deducting all expenses, including taxes and interest, from its revenue. It is calculated by dividing net profit by revenue and multiplying the result by 100. A higher net profit margin indicates that a company is more efficient in controlling its expenses.

3. Return on assets (ROA): This ratio measures a company's ability to generate profit from its assets. It is calculated by dividing net profit by total assets and multiplying the result by 100. A higher ROA indicates that a company is more efficient in using its assets to generate profit.

4. Return on equity (ROE): This ratio measures a company's ability to generate profit from its shareholders' equity. It is calculated by dividing net profit by shareholders' equity and multiplying the result by 100. A higher ROE indicates that a company is

generating more profit per dollar of equity.

5. Operating profit margin: This ratio measures a company's profit after deducting operating expenses from its revenue. It is calculated by dividing operating profit by revenue and multiplying the result by 100. A higher operating profit margin indicates that a company is more efficient in managing its operating expenses.

Profitability ratios are important because they provide insights into a company's ability to generate profits from its core operations. Investors and analysts use these ratios to compare a company's profitability with its peers and industry benchmarks. However, it's important to keep in mind that profitability ratios can be influenced by various factors, such as accounting practices, capital structure, and industry dynamics. Therefore, it's important to use these ratios in conjunction with other financial and non-financial metrics when evaluating a company's financial performance.

Chapter 3: Liquidity Ratios

Liquidity ratios are a group of financial ratios that measure a company's ability to meet its short-term obligations with its current assets. These ratios are used to evaluate a company's ability to generate cash quickly to pay off its debts and fund its day-to-day operations. Here are some of the most commonly used liquidity ratios:

1. Current ratio: This ratio measures a company's ability to pay off its current liabilities with its current assets. It is calculated by dividing current assets by current liabilities. A current ratio of 1 or higher indicates that a company has

enough current assets to cover its current liabilities.

2. Quick ratio (acid-test ratio): This ratio measures a company's ability to pay off its current liabilities with its quick assets (i.e., assets that can be easily converted into cash). It is calculated by dividing quick assets by current liabilities. A quick ratio of 1 or higher indicates that a company has enough quick assets to cover its current liabilities.

3. Cash ratio: This ratio measures a company's ability to pay off its current liabilities with its cash and cash equivalents. It is calculated by dividing

cash and cash equivalents by current liabilities. A cash ratio of 1 or higher indicates that a company has enough cash and cash equivalents to cover its current liabilities.

4. Working capital ratio: This ratio measures a company's ability to fund its day-to-day operations with its working capital (i.e., current assets minus current liabilities). It is calculated by dividing working capital by revenue. A higher working capital ratio indicates that a company has more resources to invest in its operations.

Liquidity ratios are important because they provide insights into a company's ability to meet its short-term obligations and maintain its operations. Investors and analysts use these ratios to evaluate a company's cash position and to assess its ability to withstand unexpected financial challenges. However, it's important to keep in mind that liquidity ratios can be influenced by various factors, such as seasonality, business cycles, and industry dynamics. Therefore, it's important to use these ratios in conjunction with other financial and non-financial metrics when evaluating a company's financial performance.

Chapter 4: Solvency Ratios

Solvency ratios are a group of financial ratios that measure a company's ability to meet its long-term obligations with its assets. These ratios are used to evaluate a company's ability to generate enough cash to pay off its long-term debts and to fund its future growth. Here are some of the most commonly used solvency ratios:

1. Debt-to-equity ratio: This ratio measures a company's leverage by comparing its total debt to its total equity. It is calculated by dividing total debt by total equity. A higher debt-to-equity ratio indicates that a company relies more on debt financing to fund its operations.

2. Debt-to-assets ratio: This ratio measures the proportion of a company's assets that are financed with debt. It is calculated by dividing total debt by total assets. A higher debt-to-assets ratio indicates that a company has a higher degree of financial risk.

3. Interest coverage ratio: This ratio measures a company's ability to pay its interest expenses with its operating income. It is calculated by dividing earnings before interest and taxes (EBIT) by interest expenses. A higher interest coverage ratio indicates that a company has more resources to cover its interest payments.

4. Debt service coverage ratio: This ratio measures a company's ability to pay off its debt obligations with its operating income. It is calculated by dividing earnings before interest, taxes, depreciation, and amortization (EBITDA)

by total debt service (principal and interest payments). A higher debt service coverage ratio indicates that a company has more resources to service its debt obligations.

Solvency ratios are important because they provide insights into a company's ability to meet its long-term obligations and to fund its future growth. Investors and analysts use these ratios to assess a company's financial stability and to determine its capacity to take on more debt or to issue new equity. However, it's important to keep in mind that solvency ratios can be influenced by various factors, such as changes in interest rates, industry dynamics, and economic conditions. Therefore, it's important to use these ratios in conjunction with other financial and non-financial metrics when evaluating a company's financial performance.

Chapter 5: Efficiency Ratios

Efficiency ratios are a type of financial ratio that measure how efficiently a company is using its resources to generate revenue. These ratios can provide valuable insights into a company's operations and help identify areas where improvements can be made. In this chapter, we'll take a closer look at some of the most commonly used efficiency ratios.

1. Inventory Turnover Ratio The inventory turnover ratio measures how many times a company's inventory is sold and replaced during a given period. A high inventory turnover ratio can indicate that a company is effectively managing its inventory levels and is able to quickly sell its products.

2. Accounts Receivable Turnover Ratio The accounts receivable turnover ratio measures how quickly a company is able to collect payments from its customers. A high accounts receivable turnover ratio can indicate that a company has

effective credit policies and is able to quickly convert its sales into cash.

3. Accounts Payable Turnover Ratio The accounts payable turnover ratio measures how quickly a company pays its suppliers for goods and services. A high accounts payable turnover ratio can indicate that a company is able to effectively manage its cash flow and pay its bills on time.

4. Asset Turnover Ratio The asset turnover ratio measures how efficiently a company is using its assets to generate revenue. A high asset turnover ratio can

indicate that a company is effectively utilizing its resources to generate sales.

5. Working Capital Turnover Ratio The working capital turnover ratio measures how effectively a company is using its working capital to generate revenue. A high working capital turnover ratio can indicate that a company is able to generate sales without having to rely heavily on its current assets.

Efficiency ratios can be useful for comparing a company's performance against industry benchmarks or historical performance. By identifying areas where a company can improve its efficiency, these ratios can help management make informed decisions about how to allocate resources and improve profitability.

Chapter 6: Interpreting Financial Ratios

1. Understanding Ratio Analysis Ratio analysis involves using financial ratios to evaluate a company's performance. Financial ratios are calculated by dividing one financial metric by another to provide insight into different aspects of a company's financial health.

2. Benchmarks and Industry Standards Interpreting financial ratios requires context. One way to gain context is by

comparing a company's ratios to industry benchmarks or standards. This can provide insight into how a company's performance compares to others in its industry.

3. Trend Analysis Trend analysis involves comparing a company's ratios over time. This can provide insight into a company's performance over time and help identify areas of improvement or deterioration.

4. Ratio Relationships Interpreting financial ratios also involves understanding how different ratios relate to one another. For example, a company's liquidity

ratios, such as its current ratio and quick ratio, may be negatively impacted if its debt-to-equity ratio is too high.

5. Limitations of Ratio Analysis It's important to recognize that ratio analysis has limitations. Financial ratios are based on historical financial data and may not necessarily predict future performance. Additionally, external factors such as changes in the economy or industry can impact a company's performance.

Interpreting financial ratios requires a comprehensive understanding of the company's financial statements, as well as an understanding of industry benchmarks and trends. By using ratio analysis as a tool to evaluate a company's performance and financial health, investors, analysts, and management can make informed decisions about the company's future.

Chapter 7: Limitations of Financial Ratios

Financial ratios are a valuable tool for evaluating a company's financial health, but it's important to recognize their limitations. In this chapter, we'll discuss some of the limitations of financial ratios and how to overcome them.

1. Historical Data Financial ratios are based on historical financial data and may not necessarily predict future performance. External factors such as changes in the economy or industry can impact a company's performance, making it difficult to rely solely on financial ratios for decision making.

2. Industry Differences Different industries have different financial structures and operating models. For example, a technology company may have a higher debt-to-equity ratio than a utility company due to the nature of their operations. Comparing financial ratios

across industries may not provide accurate insights into a company's performance.

3. Accounting Methods Financial ratios can be impacted by accounting methods used by a company. For example, companies may use different depreciation methods, which can impact their asset turnover ratios. It's important to be aware of the accounting methods used by a company when interpreting financial ratios.

4. Window Dressing Companies may manipulate financial ratios to make their financial performance appear better

than it actually is. For example, a company may delay paying its bills to improve its current ratio. It's important to be aware of potential window dressing and look beyond the ratios to get a true understanding of a company's financial health.

5. Limited Comparability Financial ratios can be impacted by differences in accounting standards and methods across countries. Comparing financial ratios across countries may not provide accurate insights into a company's performance.

To overcome the limitations of financial ratios, it's important to use them as part of a comprehensive analysis that takes into account external factors, industry benchmarks, and accounting methods. It's also important to look beyond the ratios and analyze other aspects of a company's financial statements to get a complete understanding of its financial health.

www.ingramcontent.com/pod-product-compliance
Lightning Source LLC
Chambersburg PA
CBHW070913220526
45466CB00005B/2202